Hypnotherapy

A Concise Guide…

Author: John Pullen

Copyright © 2013 John Pullen

Publisher: John Pullen

First EBook Edition: 2013

This Paperback Edition: 2014

Printed by CreateSpace, An Amazon.com Company

Cover Image Design: Jonathan Harvey

Available from Amazon.com, CreateSpace.com and other retail outlets

www.johnpullenwriter.com

To

London College of Clinical Hypnosis

British Society of Clinical Hypnosis

&

Dedicated to all those therapists whose single aim is to practice to the best of their ability, uphold the highest ethical standards and to always do good work for their client.

Contents

Milton Erickson

Chapter 3: How Does Hypnosis Work?

Central Nervous System

Mind Body Connection

Hypnotic Trance

Chapter 4: Why We're the Way We Are

Emotions

Traumatic Episodes

Childhood Influences

Chapter 5: Negative Feelings and Emotions

Anxiety

Fear

Guilt

Doubt

Apathy

Jealousy

Summary

Chapter 6: The Therapy Session Explained
72

Preparation

Case History

Induction

Deepening

Therapy

Ego-Strengthening

Formal Awakening

Chapter 7: How Hypnotherapy Can Help
88

Stress and Anxiety

Self-Confidence

Low Mood

Pain Management

Irritable Bowel Syndrome

High Blood Pressure

Obsessive Compulsive Disorder

Eating Disorders

Smoking

Weight Control

Phobias

About the Author

About Hypnotherapy

Introduction

The purpose behind this series of guides is to present the important facts and salient points of a subject in a clear and concise way. Each book should take the average reader several hours to complete.

However, remember that to take in all of the information will require a little more time. But the aim is still the same; to inform and entertain you about a wide variety of subjects and further titles are being added on a regular basis.

This book is about the fascinating subject of Hypnotherapy and it is recommended that you read this before reading any of the Self-Help books which are also available in this series.

After completing this book you will understand not only the principles behind hypnotherapy, but also its place in the "talking therapies". In addition, the sections covering some of the more common problems people suffer from may also give you some insight in understanding any you may be experiencing and then how to proceed in getting the right treatment. We are all different, but a lot of the worries, concerns and emotional symptoms we may encounter in life are really quite common and can be treated successfully.

After reading this book, you should have a better understanding of how you function as an individual and how you have been shaped into being the person you are. And if there are areas in your emotional life which you feel need a little attention, then read how hypnotherapy may supply the help you need to make those positive changes.

Remember to always consult your doctor if you have a condition or symptoms that are worrying you.

Chapter 1

What is Hypnosis?

What is hypnosis? It's a short and easy question to ask but the answer is not so easy and straightforward. In fact this question is often answered with a series of statements describing what hypnosis is not. For example, being in a hypnotic trance is not sleep. Nor is it being awake. It is also not being in a meditative state although in some respects the two are similar.

But for the moment let's just say that it is a state of relaxed but focused concentration. This means that the person involved is feeling very relaxed but they are still aware of their surroundings and of anything that is being said to them at the time. Although this is not a complete definition, it does encompass the major aspects of the trance state and this will help to explain later why hypnotherapy can be so effective in treating a wide variety of symptoms and conditions.

Point to Note

Hypnosis is a state of relaxed but focused concentration.

A Natural Phenomenon

One thing we can say about a hypnotic trance is that it is a natural phenomenon. In fact it may surprise you to learn that you have most likely experienced a hypnotic state on many occasions. What is more, there are a number of you who have used one of the many hypnotic procedures to, for example, relieve the pain of another person. Hard to believe? Let's look at an example of a naturally occurring state of hypnosis which answers all of the criteria of being in a hypnotic trance.

Imagine a time when you were driving down a road; a motorway would be a good example. The radio may be on or off. You may be thinking about a particular topic or nothing in particular. You're driving safely; in the right lane and at the correct speed for the road conditions at the time. If another car should pull out in front of you or if the vehicle in front applies their brakes, you react appropriately and continue to drive on safely.

After a period of time, let's say about thirty minutes, you see a sign for the junction where you intend to turn off. At this point you may notice a slight increase in awareness as you prepare to leave the motorway.

At the same time you may also begin to realise that you can't quite remember the last thirty minutes or so of driving. Perhaps you can only recall fragments of that part of the journey. But you know that you were driving safely because you were reacting to other traffic correctly. But the time seems to have slipped by.

What you have experienced is a form of natural hypnosis. Your mind was relaxed, perhaps wandering or maybe focused on a particular subject to the exclusion of other thoughts. But at the same time you were aware; aware of other road users, aware that you were driving safely and aware when it was time to "wake up" and prepare to leave the motorway.

So the hypnotic state may be described as akin to daydreaming. Now let's look at an example of how many of us have used a hypnotic procedure to help relieve the pain of another person.

All of you who have children will have experienced your child falling over or bumping into something which although not causing serious injury, does result in a flood of tears. The action of "Let Mummy kiss it better" or "Let Daddy rub it better" is often the first course of action a parent takes. And in most cases, that is all that is needed to stop the crying.

Why is this? It is because the "I've hurt myself and therefore I cry" pattern of behaviour has been broken by distracting the child with the kiss or rubbing action. Once this pattern of behaviour has been broken using distraction, the child recovers from the perceived pain and stops crying.

Point to Note

Distraction can break inappropriate and negative patterns of behaviour.

Other forms of distraction (without kissing the patient) can be used by hypnotherapists in formal therapy to help break other inappropriate patterns of behaviour such as smoking, overeating and phobias for example.

Medical Evidence

It was mentioned earlier that hypnosis is often described as what it isn't; sleep, wakefulness and meditation. The evidence for this has come from orthodox medicine in the form of new using new types of diagnosis tools such as Magnetic Resonance Imaging MRI and Computerised Axial Tomography or CAT scanners.

These machines are able to produce extremely detailed cross sectional views of the internal workings of the body. When they are focused on the brain, it is possible to see which parts of it are active and which are passive during each of these states at any particular moment.

Therefore by making scans of a person's brain whilst they are asleep, awake, in meditation and in a hypnotic trance, an examination of the images produced will show if the brain is operating in a different way for each state. The result is that the scans do show that each state affects the brain differently and so we can be fairly certain that the trance state is a unique one.

Can I be Hypnotised?

This is one of the first questions asked by those interested in the subject. The quick answer is "yes." Most people can be hypnotised to some extent. In fact some research indicates that about 85% of people can be put into a trance state.

But perhaps a more practical answer to the question is that everybody can be hypnotised to some degree if they want to be. However this is not as simple as it sounds. A person may for example, desperately wish to get rid of a phobia which is affecting their life. But they refuse to go into a hypnotic trance. There are many possible reasons for this and we shall discuss them later in this book.

But one of the commonest reasons is a fear of losing control or a belief that they are giving control of themselves to somebody else, in other words, the hypnotherapist. This results in them resisting the therapy. However, if you take a moment to remember something that was said earlier; a person in a trance state is aware of what is being said to them. Therefore the person in a trance state can always choose whether to accept or ignore any therapeutic suggestions that are given to them. If they don't feel right, don't accept them. It is as easy as that.

Point to Note

In hypnotherapy the patient is in control, not the hypnotherapist.

This is one of the reasons why a full Case History is taken before a person is placed into trance for the first time. It is during this stage that the therapist will discuss the presenting symptoms or condition with the patient and come up with an agreed form of treatment and the list of positive suggestions which are acceptable. Once again, all of this will be covered in more detail later on in the book.

Stage Hypnosis

This question of who is in control during a hypnosis session now brings us to a topic which is almost guaranteed to raise the hackles of most professional clinical hypnotherapists. It is the subject of stage hypnosis and the comparisons which are sometimes made between the two.

As part of the Case History I take with every new client, one of the questions I ask is what their present knowledge of hypnosis is. This tells me the level of detail I need to go into when explaining how hypnosis works. In the vast majority of cases the answer comes back along the lines of, "Not a lot but I have seen stage hypnosis." This is usually as a live show or on television.

My first response to such answers is to forget about what you have seen on stage or on television, clinical hypnotherapy is very different. Why do I make such a clear distinction between the two?

Throughout this book I will be emphasising the ethical approach carried out by therapists along with the attention to detail regarding the welfare of the client. I am not saying that stage hypnosis is dangerous although there have been some court cases in the past. But what I am saying is that in the therapy room, the care of the client is paramount.

There are a few medical conditions where hypnotherapy is contraindicated and a number of others where the advice of the client's own doctor should be sought and their permission given before embarking on a course of therapy. The very nature of stage hypnosis makes this difficult.

Let's take an example. If a client turns up at the surgery under the influence of alcohol I would not put them into a trance but instead counsel them and ask them to return at a later date. With a stage show taking place in a pub or bar there is every chance that alcohol will play a part in the "performance" of the subject.

Point to Note

Stage hypnosis and clinical hypnosis are very different in their approach and implementation.

I am not trying to denigrate stage hypnosis but what I am attempting to do is to say that there is a clear distinction between the two. In the therapy room, the client and their needs are respected at all times.

Chapter 2

History of Hypnosis

In the last chapter we learned that there are two forms of hypnosis around today; clinical hypnotherapy and stage hypnosis. We also discussed the fact that they do not sit comfortably alongside each other. And this state of affairs is nothing new. The history of hypnosis contains many instances where it has been primarily used as a therapeutic tool and others where the science behind it was dubious to say the least.

Earliest Accounts

One of the most surprising facts about hypnosis is that it has been around for so long. In fact it stretches back as far as the study of medicine itself. The earliest recording of the use of a technique akin to hypnosis is to be found in the Ebers Papyrus from ancient Egypt. It describes a physician placing his hands upon the head of his patient and through a variety of verbal utterances, produces a "cure."

Point to Note

Hypnosis in one form or another has been known and used as a therapeutic tool for thousands of years.

The Egyptians also built sleep temples which were dedicated to the god Isis. A patient would be put into a sleep-like state by a temple physician and then Isis would appear and heal the person with her "powers."

The idea of sleep temples caught on and accounts of them can be found in both Greek and Roman records. In Greece, the temples were dedicated to the god Asklepios. From what we can gather, the procedures were similar to those used by the Egyptians but with Asklepios healing the patient whilst they slept. In each case the "laying on of hands" seems to have been a precursor to achieving a hypnotic trance.

Further recordings of the "laying on of hands" can of course be found in the Bible and there are plenty of accounts and examples of acts of healing. Whether you believe these accounts to be literal or metaphors is a personal matter for each person. But whichever standpoint you come from, the use of sleep or trance as a means of healing seems to be well known at this time.

Meanwhile in Greece, we know that Hippocrates, the "father of medicine" was aware of the phenomenon of hypnosis. In fact "hypnos" is the Greek word for sleep and Hippocrates believed that in a sleep-like state with the eyes shut, it was possible for the "soul" to see what the affliction was.

Across the other side of the world the Chinese had also been aware of the power of words and of the movement of hands over the body. Their own "father of medicine," Wang Tai used such techniques around 2,000 BCE.

Franz Mesmer

Jumping ahead over three thousand five hundred years we come to Franz Mesmer. He was an Austrian physician and from his name we get the term "mesmerism." Arriving in Paris in 1778 he set about developing his ideas about what he called "animal magnetism." He believed that each one of us had a magnetic field surrounding our body and when it became disturbed, illnesses would manifest themselves.

Mesmer decided he could use his own body's magnetic force to put the patient's disturbed magnetic field back into balance. You may come to the belief that low self-esteem was not a problem within Mesmer. He would attempt to treat his patients by making passes over their body in order to induce trance-like states. However, in some cases this could take hours so there is the strong possibility that sheer tedium and boredom caused the patient to fall asleep or go into a "mesmeric coma."

Point to Note

Mesmer was responsible for the terms mesmerism and animal magnetism. He also attempted the first group therapy.

If nothing else, Mesmer was a showman and soon he wasn't content with just treating patients on a one-to-one basis. He decided to go into mass production or to be a bit more generous to him he developed a form of group therapy. This took the form of a machine which had a store of animal magnetism. It consisted of a large covered bath filled full of iron filings and with metal bars protruding from it. The patients would grip these bars as the treatment commenced.

Being the showman he was Mesmer designed his therapy room in a way that would impress his clientele. It was situated in the Hotel Bullion and he tried to create an air of mysticism using a combination of lighting, music and mirrors. He claimed many successes and perhaps the reason why many people felt an improvement was due to belief and expectation of a cure. Mesmer's own flamboyant nature only added to the event.

Unfortunately for Mesmer he had a defect in his own psychological make-up; he desired to be recognised as a healer, somebody to be acknowledged and someone to be applauded. Perhaps there is a similarity today as some people will appear on reality television shows with the sole intention of being "famous" for its own sake. But Mesmer also wanted to be recognised by doctors and practitioners within the orthodox medical establishment. However, this was not forthcoming.

Some were jealous of his fame whilst others did not accept his explanation of animal magnetism. They came up with a way to test out his claims. But such was Mesmer's fame that it took the formation of a Committee of Enquiry appointed by no less a person than King Louis XVI to set up the test. Mesmer was asked to magnetise a cup of water and then to administer it to a subject. This he duly did, but in the meantime, the cup was substituted by another cup containing plain water. Upon drinking the water, the subject fell into a trance state.

These days we can look at the results and discuss whether the placebo effect was present here. But for Mesmer the effect was dramatic; he left Paris in disgrace. Others jumped in and carried on his work but without all the associated trappings, props and showmanship of Mesmer.

However, in the present day, he is looked on as a pioneer of hypnosis. Yes, he was too much of a showman but perhaps his greatest fault was his inability to understand what was really going on. All of the special effects he was employing were just a method for the subject to go into a self-hypnotic trance state. The heightened belief from this experience may then have allowed them to tap into their unconscious mind in order to help themselves. Altogether, this is a more rational explanation for what might have been going on.

Point to Note

In trance, the mind becomes highly responsive to suggestions.

One of Mesmer's students who carried on his work was the Marquis de Puysegur. He brought more of a scientific view to what was happening by making careful observations of his subjects. From this he noticed that when patients were induced into a hypnotic trance state, they became highly responsive to suggestions. This discovery would become an important facet in the modern use of hypnotherapy. But more of this later.

James Braid

The term hypnosis was first put forward in 1841 by an ophthalmologist from Scotland going by the name of James Braid. There are a number of accounts of how he became interested in the study and practice of hypnosis. It is possible that they all have some basis in fact.

The first is that he was witness to a performance of mesmerism. The second to an occasion when he was late in attending to a patient of his. When he arrived, he found the person staring at a lamp in the waiting room. The patient appeared to be unaware of Braid's presence. However, when Braid spoke to him and gave him an instruction, the person blindly obeyed and carried out the suggestion.

Braid had stumbled onto another method of inducing the trance state. By getting the subject to focus their attention on an object, they appeared to slip into a hypnotic trance. With some experimentation it was Braid who gave us one of the most iconic images of hypnosis; the swinging watch.

James Esdaile

It was now only a matter of time before the study of hypnosis would be used as a method of deadening pain during surgery. And it was a young British surgeon, James Esdaile who started performing hypnosis on his patients before operating on them. There are reports that he conducted over 250 such procedures including amputation of limbs and the removal of tumours in this way.

It was only the discovery of chloroform as an anaesthetic that stopped hypnosis being used for this purpose. Well that's not entirely correct; today there are still cases now and again where the use of orthodox anaesthetics is contraindicated. On these rare occasions hypnosis has been used to great effect and success.

Point to Note

Pain can often be treated successfully using hypnosis. But the cause of the pain must first be diagnosed by a doctor before treatment can begin.

Pain can be treated successfully using hypnosis. On a personal note, some years ago I treated a lady with severe back pain due to spinal injuries sustained in a car accident. Working with her consultant and seeing her on four occasions, her pain was reduced to a point where she could control the level of discomfort herself and consequently was able to enjoy a good night's sleep for the first time in over a year without having to resort to additional painkillers and sleeping tablets.

Charcot, Liebault and Bernheim

Towards the end of the nineteenth century there were a number of new theories put forward concerning the nature of hypnosis. One of these was announced by Jean-Martin Charcot who practices as a neurologist. He believed that the trance state was a form of induced seizure where patients exhibited "hysterical" behaviour. However his theory did not stand up well to scrutiny and it was soon disproved.

The two people involved in disproving this theory were Ambroie-Auguste Liebault and Hippolyte Bernheim. Liebault's contribution was to further the idea of suggestions as part of the therapy. He was also the first person to indicate that therapy could be carried out even if the subject were only experiencing a light trance state. These conclusions remain true today.

Point to Note

Hypnotherapy can be effective even if the subject is only in a light trance state.

Bernheim was also interested in the use of suggestions during therapy. In addition, he reasoned that hypnosis should be treated from a psychological standpoint and that a lot of the showmanship

34

must be removed. Together, they were able to move hypnosis into the class of a normal phenomenon that could be used therapeutically.

Sigmund Freud

Another student of Charcot was Sigmund Freud who would later move on to develop the subject of psychoanalysis. Although he was not the first person to put forward the idea of each one of us possessing a conscious and unconscious mind, he believed that it was the unconscious that affected our behaviour.

Unfortunately, it appears that Freud was not all that adept at inducing hypnosis in individuals. So he rejected the subject and went about working on his theories of psychoanalysis. As a result of all this, as the end of the nineteenth century approached, Hypnosis started to fall into decline.

Hypnosis in War

Wars often produce necessities to either invent new things or to develop existing ideas. And so it was for the practice of hypnosis during both the First and Second World Wars. Its use as an analgesic again came to the fore and it was used both in surgery and as a means of removing general pain from the wounded.

But it was in the trenches of World War I that brought to attention another crippling condition. The constant effect of being shot at and bombed produced in many soldiers a condition that at the time was called "shell-shock." It was an illness which was not very well understood at the time. Many sufferers were accused of cowardice and then summarily executed by firing squad.

We now know that many were suffering from post-traumatic stress disorder or PTSD and as such, most sufferers have now been posthumously pardoned. However, for a lucky few, the condition was treated with hypnosis and this turned out to be an effective treatment.

Point to Note

Post-Traumatic Stress Disorder or PTSD is a condition which can affect anyone who has either experienced a trauma or been witness to one.

In later years and in recent wars and conflicts, the condition of PTSD has been recognised in soldiers returning home from battle. It can still be a devastating illness if not treated and has led to a number of suicides. Modern hypnotherapy along with other therapies now plays its part in helping patients to adjust to their trauma.

Medical Recognition

The years 1955 and 1958 mark important landmarks in the history of hypnosis. For it was in 1955 that the British medical Association or BMA recommended that hypnosis should form part of a medical student's training. Then in 1958, France made similar recommendations in the training of their future doctors. Today, nurses associated to the Royal College of Nursing can take courses in clinical hypnosis.

Milton Erickson

We now come to the person that most hypnotherapists regard as the "father of modern hypnosis"- Milton Erickson. The many and varied techniques he developed and pioneered are used by hypnotherapists the world over. His contributions have had a greater effect on the practice of hypnotherapy than anyone else.

It all started when he was a child. He contracted polio which led to him becoming paralysed. Whilst in this state, Erickson used the time to observe other people and concluded that what people said and did were usually quite different. This fuelled his interest in human psychology and he set about overcoming his own disability.

He became a qualified psychotherapist but gradually became to understand the importance of hypnotherapy in the treatment of some patients. Perhaps the core part of his techniques was in the use of "indirect suggestions."

The secret in using indirect suggestions rather than direct ones lies in the way a patient will either accept or reject them whilst in therapy. Indirect suggestions can be made in such a way as to fit in with a patient's unconscious needs. By using these techniques, he was able to bypass any natural conscious resistance to therapy that the patient might have.

Point to Note

Erickson used Indirect Suggestions in order to bypass the conscious, analytical part of the mind so that his patients could easily go into trance.

In fact he was so good at the technique that he could induce hypnosis and deliver the therapeutic suggestions in what to the subject appeared to be no more than a casual conversation. This is also a very good way of inducing trance with a person who is feeling nervous. He would adopt and change his therapy to suit the individual by changing the tone of his voice or by using metaphors or stories in order to get the subject to relate to him.

Point to Note

Good rapport with the client is the key to setting up successful therapy.

Getting a patient to relate to a particular therapist is extremely important. It is called rapport and without it, the chances of success become reduced. Erickson's approach was to model himself on them by matching the tone of their voice and their gestures without them being aware of what he was doing. This had the effect of quickly establishing rapport between them. Some of these techniques were later further developed into the subject of Neuro-Linguistic Programming or NLP.

Erickson laid down the foundations of modern hypnotherapy practice and even though he died in 1980, his techniques are still taught around the world in colleges teaching hypnotherapy.

Chapter 3

How Does Hypnosis Work?

The central nervous system or CNS consists of the brain, the spinal chord, peripheral nervous system and the autonomic nervous system. An appreciation of how they operate together will help to clarify how hypnosis works.

Central Nervous System

The brain is possibly the most sophisticated and complicated thing that has ever existed; at least as far as we know at present. It has evolved over millions of years and we can look on it as the control room that operates everything else. In fact, to be more correct, it can be described as a number of control rooms for we now understand that different parts of the brain are responsible for different functions.

Some parts such as the amygdala are very old and evolved much earlier than other parts. It is responsible for some of our emotional functions whilst more modern parts control some of our higher functioning.

The spinal chord can be found within your spinal column and it connects the brain with the peripheral nervous system. Together they pass messages to and from the brain.

The final part is the autonomic nervous system or ANS. And what differentiates this part from the rest of the CNS is that it needs no conscious thought to activate it. In fact it can be looked upon as a type of auto-pilot, keeping many of our vital systems in check and functioning correctly. After all you don't have to tell yourself consciously to remember to breathe or to keep your temperature within strict limits. It happens automatically or unconsciously.

The autonomic nervous system can be split into two further components; the sympathetic and para-sympathetic nervous systems. How do they work?

Well, you may have heard of something called the "fight or flight" syndrome. This broadly means that if we are faced with a threat, which can be real or imagined, the sympathetic nervous system can activate a whole set of bodily reactions which prepares us to take action; in other words, to fight or run away. On the other hand, the para-sympathetic component is responsible for all the feelings of calmness which you experience when you feel relaxed.

To feel emotionally steady, both of the parts of the ANS should be able to function together. If they don't, it can lead to a whole host of symptoms and negative feelings. The important point to note in all this is that we can look at our minds' and say there are two types of mind operating; a conscious mind and an unconscious mind. And this is very important in understanding how hypnosis works.

Point to Note

Our mind can be split into conscious and unconscious parts.

Mind-Body Connection

The idea of a connection between the mind and body is not a new one. But is it real? The straight answer is "yes" and it can be demonstrated by means of a simple experiment.

So if you're ready, just relax and close your eyes. But you had better finish reading this paragraph first! Think of a large slice of fresh lemon. See it clearly in your mind's eye. Now bring it closer to your mouth. Perhaps the anticipation of it is already being felt in your mouth. Now, imagine biting deep into that juicy fresh lemon. When you do I bet that most of you will have a real physical sensation of actually doing it for real. Try it now.

If you experienced the sensation of the lemon in your mouth then you will understand that the mind can exert a physical effect on your body's responses. If you think of something that scares you, you will feel some of the sensations of being anxious. Your mind is really that powerful.

Hypnotic Trance

Let's now start to put together all that we've read so far. We know that the unconscious part of our mind is powerful and through the autonomic nervous system, it controls many vital functions that keep us alive such as breathing and temperature control.

Now when a person experiences a hypnotic trance, they are usually feeling pleasantly relaxed. This activates the part of the ANS we call the para-sympathetic nervous system and it takes over from the "awake and active" sympathetic component.

The unconscious mind now becomes more prominent and there is a feature of it which allows hypnotherapy to be used effectively; namely the unconscious mind is open to direct suggestions. In the trance state, positive suggestions to help the patient adopt new healthier habits can be given. And because the unconscious does not analyse as the conscious mind does, these new healthier patterns of behaviour are accepted. That is the basis on which hypnotherapy works. It is not magic but it is still pretty amazing.

Chapter 4

Why We're the Way We Are

In this chapter we are going to look at some of the reasons we act the way we do and why we sometimes develop symptoms and conditions which can cause problems in our lives.

Emotions

Almost all of us are aware of our emotions at one time or another. There are times we feel happy and carefree whilst other occasions when the opposite is true; we feel anxious, afraid or angry. These are all examples of emotions and they are feelings which are generated in our mind. They may be the result of a situation we encounter or they may be due to a perceived situation. Both real and perceived can produce a range of emotional responses.

Now because we already know that there is a strong connection between the mind and body, these feelings can also produce physical symptoms in our body as well. So how does this come about?

When we are feeling healthy, relaxed and happy, we can say that our mind and body is in balance. This means that the chemicals that exist within us are in balance. But remember that when we are faced with a stressful situation or a perceived stressful situation, our body will produce an excess of certain chemicals and change how our systems are operating in order to prepare us for our "fight or flight."

Adrenalin can be produced and flood our body. Our digestive system may be temporarily "shut-down" and the blood supply pumped to our arms and legs. Our minds are put on high alert. If the situation is truly dangerous, then these measures can help us survive it. But when the crisis is over, then our body should be able to return to normal; back to a state of balance. In other words, the para-sympathetic nervous system will take control and return us back to a normal relaxed state.

If it doesn't then our heightened state of alertness will remain and begin to have a detrimental effect on us. Anyone who has endured a lengthy period of stress will testify that eventually you begin to suffer from a whole host of negative symptoms and feelings. And if these are not treated, it may lead to a breakdown when the mind and body says it can't cope anymore.

Point to Note

Regular relaxation through self-hypnosis can keep us emotionally balanced.

So it is important to understand our emotional state and to become aware if outside stresses are leading us to feel "on edge" over a long period of time. If we do become aware of this happening then it is time to do something about it. One of the things that can be done is to practice relaxation through self-hypnosis. A hypnotherapist can teach you to do this and if you practice it on a regular basis, you will find that many of the stresses we come across in life can be handled without medical intervention.

Traumatic Episodes

Another factor which can have long-lasting effects on our lives is whether we have suffered or even witnessed a trauma. A trauma can be described as an event which is very frightening to us. It may be an accident we are involved in or an attack or a threat. As we said earlier, soldiers returning from a conflict can often be traumatised. The effects can be varied and if you are suffering from such a condition, you should seek medical help.

It is fairly easy to be able to define a serious or life-threatening trauma. But many of us suffer "minor" traumas which can still have a devastating effect on our lives. Some of the effects of traumas can result in the formation of phobias. These are irrational fears which can affect our lives if they are left without treatment.

There are literally thousands of phobias recorded and they can come about in many ways. For example, a child being locked or trapped in a room may feel claustrophobic in later life. Or a person being threatened by a dog may develop a phobia about dogs in general. An unpleasant flight could induce a fear of flying. The list goes on.

There are a number of techniques employed by hypnotherapists that can help to relieve the symptoms of phobias and allow the person to once again encounter their fear and live their life without undue stress or anxiety. We will discuss these techniques later in this

51

book and see just how they are able to reduce the fear felt by the individual.

Childhood Influences

As children we are highly impressionable, especially from significant others. These significant others can be parents, guardians, family members, teachers or friends. But each can be an influence on how we develop as individuals. And some of these beliefs and behaviours can remain with us into adulthood.

These influences can be positive or negative. If we learn early on to respect other peoples' feelings, then there is a good chance these values will stay with us. However, a child may equally be exposed to negative beliefs and experiences. And these too may follow them into adulthood and cause problems later in life.

On one end of the scale a child might suffer both physical and emotional abuse. This can have a devastating effect on their life and can manifest itself in many ways. This sort of conduct by an adult is of course a criminal act and should be counted as such.

But there are other forms of negative learned behaviours which may not have been committed by an adult on purpose. To give an example of this, let's once again look at a typical phobia. A mother may be afraid of spiders and her negative reaction to them in front of her child may cause that child to "inherit" the same phobia which they carry into adulthood. In turn they may also influence their children and there will be a good chance that the whole cycle will be repeated.

Point to Note

Children are impressionable. Your actions may be copied and acted out.

As you can see from the few examples given, who we are and why we act in a certain way is not at all straight forward. We have many influences acting on us from very early on right through our lives. Life is full of traumas; most very small, but some will be big. All of these can exert an effect on us and all play a part in making us who we are.

Understanding which factors have influenced our life can help us to come to terms with any problems we may be experiencing. And with that information, you can if you wish, begin to adopt new healthier patterns of behaviour.

If these then are some of the ways we can adopt negative attitudes and patterns of behaviour, then in the next chapter we will examine some of the negative feelings and emotional states that can cause us problems.

Chapter 5

Negative Feelings and Emotions

There are many negative feelings and emotions that we may experience at different times of our life. They can manifest themselves as a whole host of symptoms or presenting emotional or medical conditions. But if we look closer at these problems and question a person closely as happens in taking a Case History, we may uncover an underlying cause. Or to be more precise we may find a deep-rooted self-belief which is at the bottom of the problem.

In the last chapter, we looked at how such negative symptoms and conditions could come about. Now we will look at the negative beliefs themselves. There are a number of ways to break these down and they can overlap in the way they affect us. But the following six basic beliefs can encompass most of the problems we may experience. By understanding and treating them, many of the presenting symptoms and conditions will also improve.

Anxiety

Anxiety is an emotion which we all feel at one time or another throughout our lives. It is natural to feel anxious about certain events. However some people feel anxious or are worried most of the time. In these cases it can lead to a person feeling helpless. It can also be the start of more serious illnesses.

People who are chronic worriers who are always feeling as though they are stressed out are making themselves prone to possible high blood pressure, heart attacks and depression. And because feelings of depression and anxiety can have a detrimental effect on our immune systems, it can also lead to even developing illnesses such as some cancers.

Chronic anxiety can eat away at us; happiness becomes just a memory of what life was like. And it takes a lot of mental energy to continually worry about everything. This can wear you down until you feel as though you have no strength or motivation to do anything. You can get into a rut which is difficult to get out of. And it doesn't just affect the person concerned; it can also have a devastating effect on the people around them.

Point to Note

Chronic worry can have physical effects on your mind and body.

So what is worry? It has been described as looking into the future, deciding on what could go wrong and then concentrating on that one worst aspect. The good news is that in the vast majority of circumstances, the worst case scenario never happens. So what this means is that all this worry and anxiety has just been a waste of time and energy. Don't worry yourself about the things that might happen.

So what is the direction you should take to help alleviate these negative feelings? Relaxation is the key to feeling better. Positive thinking and cognitive behaviour therapy will also allow you to see things in a better perspective; to see things how they really are. Hypnotherapy teaches you to relax and to gain that objective perspective on life.

The right amount of healthy anxiety can alert you to possible problems ahead but overly worrying about something is not going to change anything. In fact it is only stopping you from performing at the top of your game. When you think about it, there really isn't any sense in worrying about it, is there?

Fear

Fear is a very natural and valuable feeling to have. Indeed it can stop us from taking a decision that might put us in mortal danger. As a child we may be goaded by our friends to cross a railway line or to "play chicken" on a busy road. These are dangerous and stupid things to attempt and fear can be the thing that stops us. But even in these extreme examples there is a downside; you may do the sensible thing but you are then left with the taunts of the others around you saying you are scared. This is not too good for enhancing our self-esteem.

But if we look at fear in more general terms, it can be quite a debilitating factor in our lives and create further feelings that are negative. Life is or should be a journey where we continue to develop, learn new things and try new experiences. Each one of us probably has a list of the things we would like to do in the near future. It may mean putting ourselves forward for a promotion, taking up a new activity or travelling to a foreign country.

Each of these is a challenge. They mean having to change our normal routine; to break out of what feels safe and secure. Every new undertaking carries a risk, whether it is small or large. It may be physical such as taking up a dangerous sport or it may be psychological such as a promotion interview that could end in rejection and a perceived loss of face. There is risk attached and consequently we may experience a fear of going ahead with it.

Fear is something we learn from our parents, teachers, friends or significant others. When we are young we are constantly being warned that if we do that, something bad may happen. A lot of this is good advice; we learn to do things safely. But it can also set up those negative patterns of behaviour which we carry on into adulthood. We can become conditioned to fear the feeling of fear itself. When we notice that it is stopping us from moving forward in our lives, stopping us trying anything new then we have a problem that needs to be attended to.

Point to Note

"The only thing we have to fear is fear itself" Franklin Roosevelt.

So do we stop feeling fearful over new challenges; things that we would like to do but feel afraid to? The answer is that we need to learn to accept the fear. Fear is what might happen if the worst came to the worst. In the majority of cases this does not happen. Look back on your life when you tried new things; did they turn out okay in the end? And if they did, how did you feel? I bet you felt elated and your self-esteem and self-confidence received a boost. You felt really good about yourself and you may have even felt liberated.

Whatever the new challenge, weigh up the pros and cons. Just what is the worse that could happen? But is this likely? And what are the benefits? Weigh them up as well. At the end, make a decision based on the real facts. There may be some risk on what you are planning. But take a reasoned decision and if you go ahead, accept the risk is part of the deal. If you accept the fear, then you will find you are able to take on new challenges.

One final point; some activities are very risky. If you think a thing is too risky, then accept that too and don't do it. It is all a matter of balance and that is a personal thing. But don't let fear imprison you; there is a way out.

Guilt

Guilt can be a difficult feeling to understand properly. On the one hand if we commit a crime or misdemeanour, society will demand that we feel guilty about what we have done. It is also felt by many that this guilt feeling should be borne by the individual even after any retribution has been made. Therefore society will, in general, look on guilt as a positive sign that someone is repentant and perhaps more deserving of eventual forgiveness.

But the other side of the story is that guilt is a very negative feeling. It can eat away at us until we feel paralysed by it. So, one point of view sees it as being desirable for some people to display and the other that it is very debilitating and disempowering. So who is right?

Guilt comes about when we think we have done something wrong. But is that the right feeling to have? Wouldn't regret be a more appropriate response to have? If we do something wrong, we can regret our action. But if we let it fester, then the feelings of guilt will stay with us. Recognise your mistakes, make amends and feel regret over what has happened but don't allow it to become a permanent part of your psyche.

Point to Note

Regret is a more appropriate feeling than guilt.

Many people grow up with a sense of permanent guilt. Once again, many of them will have first picked it up in childhood. Only too often parents will be over critical with a child. And constant criticism can impart a feeling of being no good at anything. Some parents may make love conditional on the child achieving something or acting in a particular way. This is a very effective but not recommended way of controlling a person.

So how do we combat unhealthy feelings of guilt? The best way is to become responsible for making your own decisions and not to rely on others to tell you whether you are at fault or not. Look at a situation, be honest with yourself, take responsibility if it is your fault, feel regret at what you did wrong, make amends and then move on.

It may be an old cliché, but if you "learn by your mistakes" it is a good and healthy yardstick to utilise in life.

Doubt

Doubt like fear can be a positive feeling if used in the right context. It is healthy and sensible not to take everything we hear as true and unquestionable. Remember the old adage, "don't believe everything you read in the newspapers," or anywhere else. Quite often we hear things from other people and we question the validity of what they are saying. There is nothing wrong with doubting things you're not sure are true.

But what can be a real problem in life is self-doubt. This can be every bit as strong as doubting others, perhaps more so. Our belief in our own abilities can be extremely clouded. We may think we know ourselves but that knowledge is based quite often on other peoples' views. Yes, as in the section on guilt, our level of self-worth may be first formed in our childhood and then validated as we live our lives.

Point to Note

Doubt can be healthy, self-doubt can be unhealthy.

The same experiences which can cause guilt can also have a dramatic effect on how we view ourselves. If we feel that we are not worth much, this will be reflected in what we do and how we react to situations we encounter in our life. When we are impressionable, constant criticism can stick in our mind and we develop a low opinion of ourselves.

For example, a person with low self-esteem will probably ignore the nine times out of ten that they are praised for doing something. Then, when one person criticises them, that is all they remember and quite often, they will use a very self-critical internal voice to chastise themselves even more. In the long run, it will have the effect of confirming that they are worthless.

Because self-doubt is often a long term problem, it can be felt by the individual to be hard-wired into their personality; in other words, it's too late to be able to change. This is not true.

They may feel as though they are a permanent part of who you are but you can change. The secret is to examine why you feel this way and then look for examples to back it up. At first you will find some negative examples. But then, think a bit deeper and begin to remember all those times you were praised. Begin to doubt your own self-doubt.

Then go back to those examples you thought validated your low self-worth and really examine them closely. Were those few occasions really your fault; were there other factors at work? Perhaps you were taking the blame for something that wasn't directly your fault.

Make a real effort to allow your mind to become more flexible; to look at things in a new and more objective way. In time you will notice the difference and your self-esteem will rise.

Apathy

Apathy can be described as a lack of motivation. Everyone has days when they don't feel like getting out of bed to go to work. Others will keep putting off a task by making up the smallest of excuses not to do it. Both of these are understandable. But if this feeling of not being able to do anything begins to get out of hand and becomes the "norm" then you are likely to be harbouring feelings of apathy.

Apathy has quite a bit in common with doubt. It is underlined by a fear of failure. If you have been "conditioned" to feel that you are likely to fail in an endeavour, eventually you begin to think if you should really try to attempt it in the first place. This feeling can grow over time and begin to stop you from attempting to try anything new. You tread water in your life and fail to move forward.

Point to Note

Apathy is underlined by a fear of failure.

With this attitude eating away within you, any new challenge will appear to be harder than it actually is. You tackle it with less than your best effort, which in turn, makes it more likely that you will fail. This then validates your opinion that you should never have bothered in the first place.

The answer to changing this feeling is to alter your mind set. Whenever you take on a new endeavour, there is no guarantee that you will succeed. In fact there is a strong possibility that you may fail or not get exactly the result you are looking for. This is normal. Making mistakes is a key to learning how to do things correctly. History is filled with successful people who failed hundreds of times trying to perfect something. There is nothing wrong with failure if you understand what went wrong and you learn from your mistakes. Yes, it is yet another old saying that "we learn by our mistakes." But again it is true. Do not be put off by failure; it is the best way to learn and move forward.

Jealousy

Jealousy is another negative feeling that just eats away at us. It is a very powerful emotion. At its worst, it can destroy your health. It can lead to depression, anger, drug and alcohol dependency and eventually, it could kill you.

Jealousy can come about in lots of different ways. You may be jealous of a work colleague who has been promoted, or someone who owns a house or car that you want. And it can definitely happen to someone who has lost out on a relationship to a rival. But at its base level, it is wanting something that somebody else has and you can't. Or so you think.

The key to combatting jealousy is not to look on it as something you can't have. Instead look on it as an incentive to achieve the same for yourself. If you keep your goals realistic, at least in the short term, there may be no real reason why you can't achieve the same sort of things for yourself too.

But if you remain being eaten away with jealousy, your chances of getting what you want will take a nosedive. And breaking out of this mind set is not easy. There may be threads of self-doubt lurking here and it can act as a barrier to freeing yourself up and becoming positive and motivated to start achieving your dreams.

Some people will see themselves as "victims;" it's not my fault, I was born poor. Or I never had the same opportunities as he or she had. That may be true but it should not stop you from changing what has gone on before.

You have a choice; you can look back and blame someone else or a situation for why you have failed. Or you can turn around and look forwards and decide that what is in the past is in the past and then to decide to change your circumstances. No one is saying that it will be an easy ride but if you don't try, you are likely to stay where you are.

However, if you do decide to take that first step forwards, here are a couple of things to keep in mind. When you set your mind on something, ask yourself whether you need it or just want it. A simple enough question but the right answer can help to make your journey a whole lot easier.

If you tell yourself you need something, say a new house worth £250,000, you are immediately putting a huge amount of pressure on yourself. Of course if you are a high earner, it may not be a problem but if not, then you are making life difficult. Instead, ask yourself if your real motivation is that you would like to own that house. Here, the "need" is replaced with a "desire" and subsequently, the pressure is reduced; you can still plan and set about trying to obtain it but you are no longer under the self-imposed pressure of needing it. This is a much more healthy way of looking on things that we would like to have.

There are very few real needs in life, the rest are desires. Try to encourage your mind set to desire something rather than "I must have it." The pressure on you will be considerably reduced and you may have a more realistic chance of obtaining your goals. Often, when the pressure to have something is off, it can become easier to actually obtain it.

Summary

For many people reading this chapter it will ring a bell and they will be able to identify with one or more of these emotions and mind sets. But remember that as long as they are kept under control and you don't allow them to become an imbedded part of your life, then there is nothing to be concerned about.

However, if you feel one or other of them has taken a hold, then try some of the suggestions given. If the problem is too deep-rooted, then seek professional help. With the right support you can bring your life back into balance and enjoy it by being the person you really want to be.

Chapter 6

The Therapy Session Explained

It's now time to move on from looking at the psychological aspects of how the mind and body interacts together and how particular mind sets if left untreated, can develop into conditions and problems in our life.

In this chapter we are going to discuss how such conditions and symptoms can be treated using hypnotherapy. We're going to break down a typical hypnotherapy session (if there is such a thing as a typical session), so you will be aware of what to expect and how best to prepare for it.

Preparation

So you've decided to book a hypnotherapy session. Perhaps you debated whether to try self-hypnosis first using one of the many CDs or self-help books available. These can be a help and if they encourage you to practice relaxation on a regular basis, this is no bad thing. However, if the problem is more serious or that it has been around for a long time, then it may be better to seek help from a professional hypnotherapist. So how do you find a good one?

The best way is usually from a personal recommendation but that is not always possible. A glance into a listings book such as Yellow Pages will often present a large number to choose from. And you look at some of the long list of letters after some names, it can be quite confusing.

Point to Note

Seek out a registered hypnotherapist.

To try to make things a little easier, look for therapists who are registered with a professional society. Then check out the society's web-site to confirm all their members have undergone a suitable training course and adhere to a professional code of conduct. They should all carry public liability insurance. The British Society of Clinical Hypnosis or BSCH is one such body but there are usually others listed as well.

There are probably many questions you may wish to ask your chosen therapist and I'm sure you will find them all willing to answer them for you. However, before you book that first session, there is a question you should ask yourself. Because if the answer is "no" then you should think twice before booking. And what is that question?

It is whether you are going to see the hypnotherapist because you want help for something and not because you are being forced or pressured by someone else such as a partner. If you are not going along because you want to make those changes for yourself then the chances of success will be diminished. But if the answer is "yes" what can you expect?

Case History

A case history is usually taken at the beginning of your first session. It contains a lot of the expected questions you are used to answering such as name, address, date of birth, occupation etc.

But it will also delve deeper than that and ask you questions about your medical history, marital status including children and any current anxieties you may be experiencing other than the reason you came in the first place. On top of this you may be asked what hobbies if any, you enjoy, any childhood traumas and any other therapeutic interventions you've had in the past.

The therapist is not trying to pry into your private life but is endeavouring to build a complete picture of you so that the treatment protocol will be best suited for you and your problem. If you have any questions about what you are being asked then just ask the therapist and he or she will be happy to answer you.

After this the conversation will move on to your particular concern and the therapist will ask you a number of questions pertaining to it. You can expect such questions as "when did you first notice it" and "how it affects you" amongst others.

During this period, something else will be going on. The therapist will be building up a rapport between you both. This is because a large part of a successful therapeutic session is based on trust; trust between the client and therapist and vice versa.

Point to Note

Trust and rapport are essential to achieving a successful therapy session.

When the case history has been taken and the problem fully discussed, the therapist may then explain what the therapy treatment will entail. And that is exactly what we will be discussing in the rest of this chapter.

Induction

Induction is the name given to the first stage of putting someone into a hypnotic trance. There are many ways to achieve this and different therapists will have their own preferred methods based on you and your presenting problem. But one thing they will all have in common is that it should be an enjoyable experience.

Point to Note

Inductions and trance are pleasant experiences

You may be asked if you would like to focus your attention on to a spot on the ceiling, the wall or even your hand. You may also be asked to focus on your breathing. All of these techniques are designed to relax you and to focus your attention. Eventually you may want to close your eyes or the therapist may suggest that you do so. This all helps to enhance your state of relaxation and focused attention.

Throughout, the tone of voice employed by the therapist may change but it will still feel "right" for you. This is a further indication of the rapport that has been built up from the case history.

The therapist will be using a tone of voice that he or she feels will fit in with your own patterns of communication.

At the end of the induction phase you are likely to have closed your eyes. You will be feeling quite relaxed and your mind will be comfortably focused on something. It is now time to move on to the next stage.

Deepening

The deepening phase is intended to do exactly what it implies; to deepen the trance so that therapy can take place. Once again, there many ways of achieving this and your therapist will use one that is appropriate for you.

Progressive relaxation is one method where the individual is asked to imagine relaxing their body in stages; perhaps by thinking of a warm wave of relaxation moving up and throughout their whole body. Another involves counting down from ten to one and with each decreasing number the person feels more and more relaxed. It is usually accompanied by a visualisation of perhaps walking down a safe, wide staircase. And speaking of "safe," the therapist may at times make suggestions that you are "safe and secure." This reassurance will aid trust and allow further relaxation to increase.

Point to Note

Therapy can work for all depths of trance

Remember, you do not have to be in a deep trance state to enable the therapy to be effective. Often, a light trance state is sufficient. When the therapist is satisfied that you are in a suitable trance, he or she will begin the therapy part of the session and that is what we will look at next.

Therapy

This is the part of the session which deals directly or indirectly with the reason you came in the first place. It usually takes the form of the therapist giving suggestions to the individual which are aimed at helping the condition or relieving the symptoms. Depending on the personality type of the client, the suggestions may be direct or indirect. Once again, the therapist will have made this judgement based on the conversation and case history.

If the therapist believes the individual to be influenced by someone in authority (perhaps the good law abiding citizen who respects authority) then authoritarian suggestions may be given in a direct way and in a strong tone of voice.

On the other hand, if the person is one who does not respect authority (perhaps a free-thinker who has strong views about individuality) then a more non-authoritarian approach may be used. This could take the form of suggestions that the client "may" wish to change their behaviour or suggestions that the client themselves may uncover a way to make positive changes in their life.

Point to Note

Suggestions can be direct or indirect; authoritarian or non-authoritarian.

It is all about phrasing the therapy part of the session in a way that will best get the client to co-operate in their own treatment. There are no hard and fast rules as to the length of the therapy part of the session but it is usual to restrict the number of suggestions given. This is so the person can concentrate on making the key changes in their behaviour.

Ego-Strengthening

Like relaxation, ego-strengthening or ego-boosting is a standard part of most hypnotic sessions. It normally follows the therapy stage and comes before the formal awakening. So what exactly is ego-strengthening and what part does it play in the overall therapy session?

In simple terms it is a method designed to increase your self-confidence. And why is that important? Well if you feel more confident you will also feel more motivated to put your therapeutic suggestions to work.

Point to Note

Ego-strengthening can give you more self-confidence.

Ego-boosting can take many forms; a new non-smoker may be asked to imagine all the extra benefits of health, fitness and extra money they can now expect to enjoy. A person being treated for a particular anxiety may be encouraged to feel that they are now free of the worry that was holding them back from enjoying life.

Once again the therapist will phrase it in a way that will appeal to the individual and that fits in with the rest of the session.

In some cases, for example a person presenting themselves suffering from low self-esteem and low self-worth may find that the therapy part of the session will use ego-strengthening as the main thrust in helping them. Such people may be very self-critical and will often hear their "inner voice" talking to them in a harsh or critical tone. Boosting their self-confidence is a means of helping them to overcome these problems.

So ego-strengthening, whether used to bolster an individual's self-confidence after therapy has been carried out or if it is employed as a therapeutic tool in its own right, it is a very important part of the whole session. The final part of the session is known as the formal awakening and we shall look at this next.

Formal Awakening

Whether the individual is in a light, medium or deep trance, they still have to be brought back to a fully awakened state so that they can carry on their normal life. There are a number of ways to achieve this and it may depend on the type of therapy that was given. But in most cases it will be a count-up from say one to ten.

However, it's not as simple as that. The therapist may use the opportunity to deliver some last minute suggestions either to boost the therapy or to enhance the ego-strengthening as a person can be particularly susceptive to suggestions just before waking up. It may take the form of telling them they will wake up with a good feeling of wellbeing or that they feel relaxed but motivated to make those positive changes in their life. It depends on the client and their needs.

Making sure the individual is "fully awake" is very important; all the usual sensations should feel normal and they should also feel clear-headed. A good therapist will talk to the client to make sure that all is as it should be before letting them go.

The counting-up will also usually contain some instructions such as "at the count of 8, you will open your eyes" and "at the count of 10, you will be fully wide awake." If the therapy involved age regression or age progression, the therapist will make sure that the individual is returned to the present time and place.

After the formal awakening has taken place, the therapist will probably spend a few minutes talking about any feelings or changes you may already be experiencing. He or she may also take this opportunity to give you some "homework" to do. This may happen whether you intend to have one or more sessions. The content of the homework can vary but quite often it will start out as practicing a relaxation procedure until you feel calm and relaxed. Then the therapist may suggest some visualisation; perhaps seeing yourself in the not too distant future having made the positive changes to your life.

It is obviously up to you whether you decide to do your homework but if you do, it will have two main benefits. First, it will help to boost your therapy. For example, if you presented with stress and anxiety, then practicing relaxation can only help to keep you calm and peaceful. Secondly, like most other things in life, practice makes perfect and practicing going into a self-hypnotic trance will aid you in any future sessions.

Practicing these relaxation techniques need not take up much of your time; perhaps ten minutes a day to start. But remember to only practice it when it is safe and appropriate to do so; certainly not when you are driving or operating any machinery. This is especially important if you are listening to a relaxation or hypnotic CD. Do not be tempted to listen to it in the car.

A good time for most people is when they are going to bed; the worst thing that can happen is that you'll fall asleep. And you will always wake up from a hypnotic trance, whether self-imposed or through a therapist. We will talk more about self-hypnosis later.

Chapter 7

How Hypnotherapy Can Help

You may be already getting the idea that hypnotherapy can be used in helping and relieving a whole host of conditions and symptoms. And you would not be wrong. Clinical hypnosis has been shown to be a useful aid in helping with more conditions than you might imagine.

But if you ask the question, "what conditions can be relieved by using hypnosis" to the average person in the street, you will likely hear "stopping smoking" as the first on the list. They may add stress and anxiety reduction. Others may mention weight control. All of these answers are correct.

But we can also add phobias, irritable bowel syndrome, bulimia nervosa, pain management, hypertension, skin complaints, obsessional compulsive disorders, insomnia and some sexual disorders. And that is not the full list.

In this chapter we will identify a number of areas where certain conditions and symptoms can arise and explain how hypnotherapy may be able to help. Remember, that no therapist is allowed ever to guarantee a "cure." It is against the professional code of ethics and applies to other therapeutic interventions as well. However, a well-trained and registered hypnotherapist will be able to guide you through the expected procedures and protocols. They will also be able to give you a realistic idea on what level of success you could expect. So let's take a look at some of these areas and start with one that many of us have felt from time to time.

Stress and Anxiety

These are two subjects we touched upon earlier when we were discussing the "fight or flight" syndrome. You may remember me saying that some stress in our lives can be good for us; it helps to keep us alert when we need to be.

The problem comes about when we hold onto that stress and don't let it go. If we don't relax, then the "alert" chemicals in our mind and body do not dissipate and this stops us from returning them to normal levels and us to a state of "balance." If we stay in a high state of tension, eventually we will leave ourselves open to developing a range of symptoms and conditions which can have a very negative effect on our life.

These feelings of stress, anxiety or worry can be relieved using relaxation techniques and as we just covered in the previous chapter, hypnotherapy is very good at inducing relaxation into a person. In addition, the homework given by most therapists will include a section dedicated to reaching a relaxed state of mind and body.

Point to Note

Make relaxation through self-hypnosis a regular part of your life.

Very often, when we are suffering from too much stress, we find it difficult to be objective. We can feel as if we are not in control of our own life. Hypnotherapy can help you to re-gain this objectivity. It should help you to take a step back and allow you to see things in a better perspective; to see things as they really are and not how our stressed minds may think they are.

In other ways, therapy can help you to see your situation not only as it really is, but also to view it in a more positive way. This is termed "reframing" and it is a very effective means of treating various forms of anxiety.

But the key to maintaining healthy stress levels is to understand how to build relaxation into your life and then to practice it on a regular basis. Once again, self-hypnosis can be the long-term solution to stress and anxiety control. And it can be effective even if you have suffered for many years. So there is no excuse; if you are suffering from undue stress and worry, seek help and make relaxation a big part of your life.

Self-Confidence

Self-confidence is a difficult feeling to define accurately. Many people may say that they can see it in others and at the same time, feel that they lack it in themselves. But it is more complicated than that. A person may appear to others to be at the top of their game and very self-confident but if questioned, they may admit that they actually feel the opposite. Therefore, self-confidence is subjective and can mean different things to different people.

So why do some people feel really good about themselves and others un-liked and not very capable? Well the old story of conditioning may be to blame. If an individual was brought up in an environment where they were criticised on a regular basis or were just not encouraged in the things that they tried, it is quite possible that they will not feel positive and confident in themselves and will not want to attempt new challenges.

As they get older they may begin to change their "inner voice" from one where it can be heard as an encouraging and supportive aid to one that is in itself critical of them. Take a moment now to consider what tone your inner voice uses. Perhaps think back to a time when you made a mistake. How did you think of yourself at the time?

Maybe you thought along the lines of, "I got that wrong but I know why and at least I'll know in the future what to do next time."

Or perhaps it was more like, "You stupid idiot. You screwed up and now everyone is going to know how useless you are."

Pretty different reactions to the same situation aren't they? The former acknowledges the error but is positive and constructive in the words and tone of voice it uses. From this, the person is likely to be able to move forward knowing they have learned a new lesson which will help them in the future. However, the latter reaction is only likely to lead to self-recrimination and a feeling of self-loathing. I know which one I would prefer to hear.

Point to Note

Changing our inner voice can make a big difference to how we feel about ourselves.

Hypnotherapy can help you to change the tone and content of your inner voice. It can help change it from being your worst critic to being a good friend who is there to help you in times of need. That sounds a much healthier way to think doesn't it?

Another method of increasing your self-confidence and feel-good factor is by using a procedure called "Self-Image Re-programming." In the trance state, the therapist will suggest that you see in front of you a new version of you in the near future. This "new you" is profiting by the success which your treatment has had. In other words, if you went to therapy in order to feel more confident, then the new you will appear to be confident. All the outward signs will be there; how they stand, how they look, how they conduct themselves with other people and how they sound.

Then the therapist may suggest that in your imagination, you step inside the new you and become one person. Having done this, you are immediately able to see through the eyes of the new you, you can hear through the ears of the new you and very importantly, you feel just how great it is to be the new real you. It is a technique that really works.

There is another procedure which borrows a part from Neuro-Linguistic Programming or NLP. Within NLP there is method called "modelling." This is where the individual may model their actions on another person. If the other person is opposite them and it is executed correctly, it can lead to a greater rapport between the two.

Point to Note

Model yourself on someone you admire.

But we can take it further and suggest that the individual imagines taking an attribute from a person they respect and admire; it can be someone they know or even a celebrity. When they absorb this attribute into their own personality, it can have quite an effect on how they feel and act.

If you have the time now and it is safe and appropriate to do so, then relax, close your eyes and think of a person you really admire. Get to know them in your mind and then bring that attribute out of them and into you. Then feel how different you feel and imagine yourself in different situations acting in the way your new attribute allows you to behave. The more you practice this, the more you will be like it in real life. Remember, practice makes perfect.

The more you "act out" being this new person, the clearer it will become in your mind and the more it will become you.

Low Mood

Feeling a bit down from time to time is a natural part of life. We might like to think that nothing bad is going to happen to us but inevitably it will in one form or another. Life will throw problems and disappointments at us now and again and some will be more serious than others. We may lose our mobile phone, wallet or purse. At the time each of these will cause us some stress and we are likely to end up feeling down and fed up at what has happened. And this is quite understandable. In the majority of cases the low mood associated with the loss will be temporary.

At the other end of the scale, it is quite likely that a few times in our lives we will be confronted by the death of someone close to us. The loss experienced in such cases is of course much worse and the feelings associated with it will be more severe. It will take much longer for us to come to terms with this type of loss.

In between these examples are other life events which can leave us feeling low in spirit for various periods of time. These events could include losing your job, getting divorced or having a prolonged illness. But the one thing they all have in common is that an event was the trigger which caused the low mood or depression to develop. The term used to describe this condition is "reactive depression." It is the event itself which causes the condition and feelings.

However, this is only half of the story. It is not only the event itself that can cause us to feel depressed or low, but just as important, is how we perceive the event. Let me explain by using the following example.

Imagine an office where Fred and Joe work. One day their manager comes in and announces that the chairman of the company is paying a visit tomorrow and will be calling in to see their office. Both of them go home that evening with different feelings about the day ahead. Fred doesn't get much sleep thinking about the visit. He is worried that the chairman might see something he doesn't like and fire him. Joe doesn't get much sleep either. He is excited at the prospect of being given the chance to impress the boss and maybe get a promotion in the future.

Both Fred and Joe miss a good night's sleep. Both of them have been given the same information. Fred's reaction is anxiety and worry whilst Joe's reaction is to feel excited at the prospect. The difference between them is their perception of the situation.

Point to Note

Our perception of an event can be just as important as the event itself.

And perception is so important in life. Some people get swallowed up in depression and low mood whilst others will view it as a challenge and an opportunity to turn it to an advantage. The curious thing is that both of them have shown similar symptoms. This can indicate to us that on one level anxiety and excitement can be two different sides of the same coin.

If we can find a way to view some problems that crop up in life in an objective way and try to find the "silver lining in the clouds," then we should find that we can keep our low moods to a minimum. Hypnotherapy can help in a number of ways using techniques which give the individual a new perspective on a situation or to help boost their confidence in being able to cope with adversity.

Before we finish this section, it is important to note the difference between reactive depression and clinical depression. The latter is a far more serious condition with the symptoms being more severe and lasting for much longer. If you feel that you may be suffering from clinical depression, you must immediately seek medical help and go to see your doctor. The treatment protocols are different and needs to be administered by your GP or other specialised medical professionals.

Pain Management

Pain can be a difficult subject to quantify. It is very much a subjective experience. One person's excruciating pain is another's troublesome ache. But for anyone troubled by pain of any description; after time, it can become a big problem.

Pain can be described as being of two types;-

Acute pain where the effects last over a relatively short period of time and

Chronic pain which lasts for much longer.

Both types can span the spectrum between mild and severe.

You are probably already aware that pain can also appear in different forms; from an ache to a sharp pain and almost everyone can tell the difference between them. It is also very easy in most cases to pin-point the area which is causing you pain. Or is it? You may, for example, bump your knee and feel the pain from that area. But what you are actually experiencing is a message from the pain receptor in a part of your brain which tells you that you have damaged yourself and it hurts.

Therefore, if pain is treated using hypnotherapy, the emphasis will be on the mind and changing the individual's perception of the pain; perhaps altering the perceived sensation to be one of a tingle rather than pain. The therapist will rarely take the pain away and there is a very good reason for this.

Pain is a warning. It happens when we have either damaged ourselves or there is something happening within the body which shouldn't be and it is the body's way of warning us to get it checked it out.

Point to Note

Always remember that pain is a warning that something is wrong.

One final point and this is also important. A good therapist will not treat you for pain management unless you have had it diagnosed by a doctor. Because pain is a warning, it may be trying to tell you that something serious has happened. Take for example, a headache. Most headaches are due to stress of one sort or another and hypnotherapy can help to relieve it. However, in very rare cases, it could be an indication of a tumour. Remember, I said in very rare cases; the vast majority are not serious but you must always get it checked out by a doctor first.

Irritable Bowel Syndrome

Irritable bowel syndrome or IBS for short is one of those cover-all terms which can encompass a number of symptoms. In general it can refer to such symptoms as diarrhoea, constipation, wind, abdominal pain, vomiting and general feelings of being uncomfortable within the digestive system. A person suffering from IBS may experience any one of these symptoms or a combination of them.

If you suspect that you might be suffering from IBS, get checked out by your doctor first. Although very unlikely, these symptoms could indicate other conditions.

One of the most effective ways of treating IBS is to use a multi-faceted approach which may include your doctor as well as your hypnotherapist. In some cases I have worked on, it can also include the services of a dietician. This is because the different symptoms may require a particular treatment protocol.

For example, a dietician may make out a diet-plan because certain foods may be responsible for irritating your digestive system. In addition, your doctor may prescribe medication to aid digestion and to smooth out the operation of your bowels.

That leaves the hypnotherapist. His or her role can help in a number of ways. One of the reasons why a person may develop IBS is because of our old "friends" anxiety and stress. So right away, hypnotherapy can help an individual to discover relaxation and homework in the form of practicing relaxation is important in the long-term success of the treatment.

If a person is suffering from a particular condition such as loose bowel movements or constipation, the hypnotherapist can help by means of visualisations whilst the individual is in a trance state.

Point to Note

Visualisations can often help in relieving the symptoms of IBS.

If the problem is diarrhoea, then imaging your digestive system as a river which becomes blocked can help to relieve the condition. On the other hand, if the problem is constipation then a similar visualisation of a river which flows freely may relive the condition.

Although IBS can be wide-ranging in the way it presents itself, treatment is straight-forward and shown to be effective in most cases.

High Blood Pressure

High blood pressure is also known as hypertension (whereas low blood pressure is termed hypotension) and affects a large number of people. It is a something which should not be ignored as it can lead to many serious conditions including heart attacks and strokes. It is recommended that you have your blood pressure taken by a clinical professional at regular intervals and if found to be high, follow the advice of your doctor.

Point to Note

Get any suspected hypertension diagnosed by a doctor first.

However, in addition to any lifestyle advice and or medication from your doctor, you can also use hypnotherapy to relieve some of the conditions which may underlie the hypertension. The main one is lowering tension and stress. As we have seen from earlier sections, hypnotherapy is very good at relieving stress. A few sessions with your therapist can teach you to use self-hypnosis on a regular basis, thus allowing you to control your own stress and anxiety levels.

But remember to first get the condition diagnosed by your doctor, follow any advice he or she has to offer and then to see a therapist in order to help you to lower and control some of the underlying reasons that may be responsible for your high blood pressure.

Obsessive Compulsive Disorder

Obsessive compulsive disorder or OCD is a condition that many people may be affected by in a mild form from time to time. For example, you may find yourself checking that you've locked the front door even though deep down, you know you already have. But there is a persistent worry at the back of your mind that says you'd better check it again just to be sure.

Or you may be somebody who "touches wood" for luck. On its own that may not be unusual but it is if you feel compelled to do it. These small behaviours or rituals can in some people, grow out of control until they seem to take over parts of their lives. An individual may then possibly be diagnosed as suffering from a more serious form of OCD.

So what exactly is OCD? As its name implies, it is made up of two components;-

The obsessive thought and

The compulsive ritual or behaviour that is carried out in order to suppress the obsessive thought.

The condition has its roots in anxiety and worry. But there may be many reasons why it might suddenly start to affect someone. A fearful thought may lodge itself in the mind and slowly begin to grow in intensity. Naturally our instinct is to get rid of the thought and sometimes we might do something which we think at the time may lessen it.

Point to Note

Anxiety is often the root cause of an OCD.

If our chosen action works we feel better until the thought returns. We repeat our action but find that soon it is no longer as effective as it first was. Before we know it, it has escalated into a time-consuming ritual or series of actions which also lose their effectiveness forcing us into a circular pattern of obsessive thoughts and compulsive behaviour.

OCDs can be a secretive condition; many people feel ashamed and try to hide it away. In most cases, it only makes the whole thing worse. So what can be done?

Once again, hypnotherapy has been shown to be an effective aid in helping to treat people suffering from OCDs. One of the treatment protocols is a form of Parts Therapy where the individual is put into a trance and then asked to find or identify a "part" of them which may be responsible for the problem.

Once identified, the "part" responsible is helped in whatever way is appropriate for it and then re-integrated back into the individual where it can now adopt a new role in helping rather than hindering the person concerned.

When this has been accomplished, the therapist can then concentrate on removing some of the symptoms associated with the problem.

Eating Disorders

There are a number of eating disorders but in this section we will concentrate on the one that hypnotherapy can help with. This is called bulimia nervosa and there are two different types; purging and non-purging.

The condition usually involves the patient overeating, known as binging and then getting rid of the food by either vomiting, taking laxatives or exercising in the extreme. The purging type accounts for the first two whilst the non-purging is covered by the exercise regime. In each case the person suffering from the problem will probably appear to be of normal weight. So why will an individual develop the condition?

Point to Note

There are two types of bulimia; purging and non-purging.

In many ways bulimia nervosa is similar to our last section about OCDs. Both can have their roots in anxiety and worry and both can involve a part of the patient that has been dissociated. It is the anxiety that causes some people to binge on food to a point where they just cannot eat anything else. This is a lot more than just eating a bit too much.

At this stage the person may feel ashamed and guilty at what they've done. To lessen these feelings they find a way to undo what they've done. So they purge themselves as described above or use excessive exercise to counteract the food. This is why they often appear to be of normal weight.

Another similarity to OCDs is that the sufferer will do their best to hide their condition from family and friends.

Hypnotherapy can help in a number of ways but the individual must see their doctor first in order to get a firm diagnosis. As with OCDs any hypnotherapy may take place in conjunction with help from the doctor or other medical professionals.

Because the cause may lie in issues of anxiety and low self-esteem, hypnotherapy can address them in ways similar to the conditions of stress and low confidence. Parts therapy to help with the dissociated part can also help along with suggestions to make the person aware of when they are about to eat. This conscious awareness can help them to realise what they are doing. This is important as often the binge part of the condition involves the person feeling dissociated and therefore not fully aware of their actions.

But remember once again to get a firm diagnosis from your doctor before going to a therapist. A good registered hypnotherapist will always ask permission to consult your doctor if the presenting condition warrants it. Finally, a multi-layered approach combining different medical professionals can often be the most effective way to recovery.

Smoking

If you ask somebody to list the conditions they believe that hypnotherapy can help with, then smoking is likely to come near the top of the list. It is the issue most commonly associated with clinical hypnosis and it is true that a sizable proportion of cases seen by most therapists are for stopping smoking. The vast majority of people now understand how dangerous smoking can be to our health and consequently, a large proportion would really like to be able to give it up.

Depending on the experiences you might hear about, this can be easy or hard and just about every other stage in between. A lot of people say that they have failed or not even bothered because they do not have the willpower to stop. If you fall into this category, remember that there is a difference between willpower and wanting to stop.

Hypnotherapy has been shown to be an effective means of breaking the smoking habit and in many cases, it only takes one session. That's right you read it correctly; one session. You don't need willpower to succeed. But you do need to bring something to the therapy session and that is the personal motivation to want to quit. What is important here is that it is you that wants to stop. It's no good turning up at the therapy session and telling the therapist that your partner sent you; you have to want to do it for you.

Point to Note

You don't have to have willpower but you do need to want to give up.

However, if you do have the personal motivation then hypnotherapy could be your key to a non-smoking future. But first, let's look at smoking and how it has a grip on some people. There are essentially two ways it does this. It is addictive and it is also a habit. Put together, this becomes quite a powerful combination. But it can be broken.

The addictive part of smoking comes from the nicotine absorbed by the body. This is a strong drug but what most smokers don't realise is how long it stays in the body after you've quit. The answer is twenty four to thirty six hours. Not that long at all. So why do we still feel a craving?

Point to Note

Smoking is both an addiction and a habit.

It is partly down to the second component and that is the habit. If you think about it, there are triggers to lighting up a cigarette. It might be with a drink (when you could smoke in a pub) or when you finish a meal or watching TV. You probably don't even consciously think about it; the trigger is pulled and you automatically (or unconsciously) put a cigarette to your lips. This unconscious action is obviously a key indicator why hypnotherapy can be such an effective means of stopping as it deals with the unconscious mind.

At the start of your session the therapist will take full case history and will also ask about your smoking habit. For example, when did you start, how many do you smoke and very importantly, when do you smoke? They will make out a smoking diary. The exact form of therapy will depend on the individual but there are some general principles and methodologies.

Point to Note

There are many real benefits in becoming and staying a non-smoker.

The therapy is overall very positive and upbeat with suggestions of the benefits of being a non-smoker. Your personal triggers will be addressed allowing you to not feel the need to smoke at these times. There may also be a part of the session called aversion therapy where you associate a cigarette with a smell or taste of something you find unpleasant. Combined, these techniques will cover most eventualities and give you a very good opportunity to quit once and for all.

Before we finish this section, there are a number of questions people ask which worries a number of them. Many are concerned they will put on weight when they give up. This is substituting food for the cigarettes you once had. Others wonder what they will do in times of stress when they would normally light up. The act of smoking increases the effects of stress within your body. And a number worry about any withdrawal symptoms that may appear.

The answer to all these and any others you might be concerned about will be addressed by your therapist during the session. All of these worries can be treated and are on a regular basis. Remember, if you feel the time is right for you to stop smoking, then what is stopping you? A new happy and healthier lifestyle awaits you.

Weight Control

For most people, weight control means losing weight and not trying to gain it. Although there are a few cases of the latter the vast majority of people seeking help in controlling their weight, want to lose it. And that isn't surprising. The increase in obesity in the Western World over recent years is causing concern in many medical circles.

Being overweight doesn't just put a strain on your joints it puts a strain on your heart and other vital organs. If you are seriously overweight and do nothing about it, you are a time-bomb waiting to explode.

Point to Note

Obesity can lead to many serious health problems in the future.

For too long many people have succumbed to the temptations and consequences of living in the modern world. Take-away food may taste lovely and requires very little effort to obtain it. But most of them are full of fat and high in calories. Match that with less need to exert ourselves in our daily lives and we literally have a recipe for disaster in the future.

The really crazy thing is that over the same period of time the number of new diet plans coming onto the market has increased enormously. So why isn't everybody's weight coming down? Could it be that dieting on its own isn't very effective? Rather than me making the obvious assumptions, why don't you?

Yes, the answer is straight-forward. The vast majority of people who go on diets eventually put all the weight they lost back on. Diets generally don't work over the long term. So why is that?

Many diets can be effective whilst you are on them but they only rely on you restricting the amount and type of food you eat. As soon as you reach your target weight or as close as you're going to get at that time, you usually go back to the old eating habits and patterns of behaviour. Perhaps you've already guessed why this section follows on from the one on smoking?

Excessive weight gain is caused by not only eating too much of the wrong foods but is also a habit that may have developed to compensate for other problems in our life. Three quite common reasons are stress, boredom and loneliness.

Therefore the long-term solution to weight control lies in re-educating ourselves not only to eat more healthy meals but also to change any bad eating patterns we may have developed. In some people, eating can be an unconscious habit brought on by triggers just as in smoking. And we already know that hypnotherapy can be an effective treatment in changing unhealthy habits and patterns of behaviour.

Point to Note

Changing your eating patterns can lead to permanent weight loss.

A therapist will look closely at your eating patterns and later, when in trance, make positive suggestions which will help to change them into new healthier eating patterns.

Phobias

Many people suffer from one phobia or another but in the majority of cases it does not pose any great problem. But for some, it can grow into a condition which can have a serious effect on a person's day to day life. So what exactly is a phobia and how can it come about?

A phobia is an irrational fear and it can literally be caused by just about anything. There are thousands of phobias recorded from common ones such as fear of flying or spiders to other less common ones such as a fear of clowns, feathers or the wind on your face. You may be wondering how some of these can have an effect on daily life?

Point to Note

You can develop a phobia about anything.

But if we take the last one as an example, it is one I treated some years ago. The individual had a phobic response from feeling wind or a breeze on her face. It was long-standing and had developed to the point where she could not use the London Underground system as approaching trains tend to send a steady stream of wind onto the platform as they approach. I am happy to record that after treatment, she no longer has this problem. But the point I wish to make is that even some obscure sounding fears can affect us on a daily basis. So they should be taken seriously.

Now you may say that some fears are rational and you would be right; after all, you wouldn't put your hand into a box containing a big poisonous spider? Well, I wouldn't. This is an example of a rational fear. It makes sense not to get that close to a dangerous creature. And if the thought of actually doing so brings on the symptoms of fear such as feeling nauseous and shaking, then most of us would understand that reaction.

But if you were flicking through a book and came across a picture of the same type of spider, how would you react? It is understandable if the picture made you jump a bit and also, having seen it, you decide to move on to another page.

Point to Note

Is your fear rational or irrational?

However, if the picture induces the same level of fear and symptoms as facing the real thing then this behaviour is not rational and may be indicative of a phobia. So what can cause a phobia to develop?

There isn't an easy answer to this as they can start or be triggered from a whole variety of situations. However, one of the common factors involved is that the individual is often experiencing a period of stress and anxiety. And we already know that stress can arise from many, many scenarios.

To complicate matters even further, you can also "catch" a phobia from another person. If we go back to the example of the spider phobia or arachnophobia as it is termed, a person may have learned to fear spiders from somebody else. Remember the case of a mother who is afraid of spiders passing on these fears to her children?

Another reason that may be responsible for developing a phobia can be down to experiencing a traumatic episode. Let me illustrate this with another example from my files. I once saw someone who was afraid to travel on the London Underground. This is not the same person from earlier who had a fear of wind on their face. In this instance, the man concerned had had a traumatic incident happen to him on a tube train in the past. It happened when the train he was travelling on got stuck in the tunnel.

Now this prospect isn't pleasant for anyone but in his case, he had another problem; he needed to use the toilet. As the pressure built up in his bladder, so did the anxiety. Luckily for him the train started up again and he was able to leave at the next station.

But the harm had already been done. Over time he began to worry more and more about being trapped in a tunnel aboard a train and needing to relieve himself. The fear and anxiety built up until he was terrified of getting on a tube train. This was a particularly difficult problem for him as he needed to commute by train each day to go to work. The good news is that after treatment, he is now able to relax on his daily trips to and from work. So how will a therapist treat a phobia?

As with all initial sessions, a full case history will be taken. This will include a detailed look at your particular phobia and you will be asked questions such as, do you remember how it started, what are your specific triggers, how it affects you and so on.

The objective of therapy is to bring your phobic response under control so that you will be able to encounter it without all the negative feelings and symptoms that have built up. And there are a number of procedures that can help accomplish this.

Point to Note

The purpose of treatment is to bring the fear under your control.

A common one is called hypno-desensitisation. It involves being taken into a relaxed state in trance and then visualising your particular fear. However, the key to this therapy is that you are introduced to your fear in small stages. The therapist will have already made out a SUD scale which lists your levels of anxiety in order of severity. So for the spider phobia, the picture of a spider would be nearer the low end of the scale and putting your hand near a spider would be very much near the top end.

When you are happy and relaxed about visualising a particular level of disturbance, the therapist will move you on to the next level up. You will not be moved up until you can cope with the current level. This type of therapy may need several sessions to move through your particular SUD scale but it is a tried and tested method of treatment which has been shown to be effective for many people.

Another common method of treating a phobia uses dissociation. The individual visualises themselves in a cinema watching a film starring them and encountering their phobic fear on the screen. As the process continues, the therapist guides the person through a series of actions within their visualisation that can have the effect of breaking the connection between cause and phobic response. In some cases the phobia is brought under control very quickly.

There are also other methods; one of which is called Eye Movement Desensitisation and Reprocessing or EMDR for short. Although not strictly a form of hypnosis, many therapists are trained in its use and find it a valuable tool in treating many problems.

Point to Note

EMDR is not hypnosis but many hypnotherapists use it as a treatment.

But the important point is that you do not have to suffer or put up with the very real problems associated with having a serious phobia. There is help on hand and your therapist will be able to suggest the best method for you.

At this point you may be thinking that hypnotherapy is some wonder technique that can cure almost anything. This is a wrong assumption. No registered therapist will guarantee to cure you. It is against ethics to make such claims. But hypnotherapy can be a very effective way of tackling a whole host of conditions and symptoms.

The list above is not exhaustive; there are many other conditions where clinical hypnosis can be helpful in bringing relief. Contact your local registered therapist and they will be able to offer advice about what is concerning you.

In the next chapter we will look at how you can help to ensure that any treatment remains effective and long-lasting. We will also examine what changes you can make to your life in order to feel fitter, healthier and more relaxed and positive about your life in general.

Chapter 8

Maintaining Success

We are all unique individuals and any benefit we derive from hypnotherapy treatment will also be dependent on how we live our lives in the future. A person who is treated for smoking cessation is quite likely not to want to smoke after just one session. But when they leave the therapy room, they are still going to be confronted by other people who smoke and from time to time they might even think about having a cigarette.

But don't worry; the treatment takes all of this into account and the individual will soon find that their thoughts just move onto something else. To help achieve this, the therapist may have made post-hypnotic suggestions to the person to maybe have a sip of cool clear water if they find their hands and mouth would like to have something to do. In these circumstances, the individual should obey these new positive urges.

Why? Because "practice makes perfect;" the more we carry out our new positive patterns of behaviour, the more it will become "hard-wired" into our minds and become second nature to us. This approach applies to most conditions. As part of the treatment, the therapist may give homework in the form of self-hypnosis which will help to relax you and ward off any new feelings of stress and anxiety.

Point to Note

Learn to develop new positive habits in your life.

In addition, these self-hypnotic trances can include visualisations where the individual can see themselves as acting out their lives in a more positive way. They may visualise themselves as slim and feeling fit or they may see themselves as being totally relaxed in a previously stressful situation.

Point to Note

Hypnotherapy is not magic but its effects can be amazing.

The important thing to realise is that hypnotherapy should be looked upon as the start of a new healthier chapter in your life. A life which now includes time for you to relax, take stock and reinforce all the positive suggestions made to you in therapy. Trance helps you to change your life by adopting more positive thoughts and behaviour patterns which will help to keep you relaxed, happy and balanced in your day to day life.

Perhaps all this talk of carrying on treatment after the formal sessions is making you think that maybe hypnotherapy is not a great "cure-all?" Well, I've got news for you, you are absolutely right. No therapist should ever talk about being able to cure you of any particular condition you might be presenting with. And this doesn't only apply to hypnotherapists it applies to doctors and all other medical professionals. It is not professional or ethical to talk of or guarantee a cure.

However, a vast number of procedures, medications and various therapies help millions of patients every year. And hypnotherapy is no exception. As we have seen in this book, there are many conditions and symptoms that seem to respond well and can aid recovery. But we can never guarantee it.

If we take the example of a person who has had a course of hypnotherapy to lose weight; the therapy is likely to have had the effect of changing some of the negative eating patterns they had before. But there is always the chance of falling back into the old habits. However, if the person is proactive in their continuing self-treatment, they will find that the chances of long-term success can be very much increased.

Point to Note

Hypnotherapy can HELP you to achieve success.

Be realistic in your on-going treatment. Remember that some issues you may have may have been there from childhood and are very deep rooted into your psyche. It can take time and effort on your part to achieve and maintain success. But it is worth it. If you bother to think about it at all, doesn't the idea of living your life in a more positive way make a lot of sense?

If treatment results in you adopting healthier eating patterns your body will thank you for it and you will feel a lot fitter. And if you are in a state of mind that recognises the early stages of stress and anxiety and you have the tools to stop it before it gets out of hand, then surely that is a goal worth aiming for. Life should be about feeling healthy and fit. It should be about feeling calm and relaxed most of the time. And finally, you should be happy and positive about where you are and where you are going. Combined, they should allow you to live your life by being the person you really want to be.

Final Point to Note

Live your life by being the person you really want to be.

Further Information

For further information about the author, go to

www.johnpullenwriter.com

For further information and resources about hypnotherapy, go to;-

www.hypnohealthservices.com

For information about training to become a hypnotherapist, go to;-

www.lcch.co.uk

Other Books by the same Author

Non-Fiction

Aviation Series

How to Fly a Plane

The Private Pilot Flying Course Part 1

The Private Pilot Flying Course Part 2

The Private Pilot Skill Test

The Flight Pilot Radio Manual

The Flight Pilot Instrument Rating Flying Course Part 1

The Flight Pilot Instrument Rating Flying Course Part 2

Medical Series

Hypnotherapy

Being Happy

Stop Smoking

<u>History Series</u>

Secret London Churches

Secret London Places

<u>Fiction</u>

Dragon's Claw

Dark Angel

Rogue Knight

All available through Amazon

Search "John Pullen" on www.amazon.co.uk